MW00423256

THEN & NOW

MARIETTA REVISITED

OPPOSITE: Marietta recovered from the devastation of the Civil War by the time this drawing was made in the mid-1880s that depicts the west side of the square. The original drawing was featured on the cover of an 1887 booklet published by the Western and Atlantic Railroad (W&A) touting northwest Georgia. (Courtesy of Marietta Museum of History.)

THEN & NOW

MARIETTA REVISITED

Joe Kirby and Damien A. Guarnieri

Joe Kirby dedicates this book to his wonderful wife, Fran,
children, Lucy and Miles, and the readers of the Marietta Daily Journal.

Damien A. Guarnieri dedicates this book to his wonderful wife, Lisa,
and his son, Luke, for their love and patience;
and to his family and friends for their support and encouragement.

ON THE FRONT COVER: The Strand Theatre was the jewel of Marietta Square when it opened in 1935 and for many years after before falling into disrepair. It now has been restored and reopened in early 2009, bringing a taste of art deco elegance to downtown Marietta. (Then image courtesy of Marietta Museum of History; now image courtesy of Damien A. Guarnieri.)

ON THE BACK COVER: Whitlock Avenue has changed greatly since this photograph was taken during World War II. The furniture store is now a pizzeria, the car dealership is a theater, and the newspaper office is now a museum. (Then image courtesy of Marietta Museum of History.)

CONTENTS

ACKNOWLEDGMENTS

As with the previous books we have written, this one would not be possible without the work of the past and present local historians, both professional and amateur. Once again, special thanks must go to founder Dan Cox and director Jan Galt Russell of the Marietta Museum of History. The contributions of the museum's Anna Monroe, who also scanned numerous old photographs, were invaluable to us.

A large part of the photo archive at the museum began as the collection of *Marietta Daily Journal* associate editor Bill Kinney, a fixture at the newspaper and of Cobb County journalism since the late 1930s. Kinney's career has touched parts of eight decades and was still progressing as this book was being written. Kinney was a proverbial font of knowledge when it came to identifying "what was what" in some of these photographs and offered unexpected insights into many of them.

Thanks are due, too, to those who loaned photographs or let us scan copies of their collections, including Kinney, *Marietta Daily Journal* (*MDJ*) publisher Otis A. Brumby Jr., Kennesaw State University (KSU) professor Dr. Tom Scott, the KSU Archives, Guy "Buck" Northcutt Jr., Aymar Manning, Wilder Little, and Philip Goldstein. A word of appreciation is due as well to *MDJ* chief photographer Thinh D. Nguyen for the timely—and lengthy—loan of a lens and to *MDJ* newsroom clerk Damon Poirier for voluntarily scanning photographs and burning discs for us on his own time. And a thank you to Strand Theatre director Earl Reece for his enthusiastic cooperation in regards to our cover shot and to Goldstein for allowing us up on the roof of the old First National Bank Building in order to try to recreate the picture on the cover of the 1887 W&A Railroad booklet.

And finally, special thanks are deserved for Dan Cox, Dr. Tom Scott, Kinney, and Joe's wife, Fran, for proofing this manuscript as they have done on our previous ones.

INTRODUCTION

We shape our buildings, and afterwards, our buildings shape us.

—Winston Churchill

Marietta, Georgia, has shaped its share of memorable buildings in its 175 years. These buildings, in turn, have helped shape those who have lived and worked here. And some of those buildings—or their memories—continue to shape Marietta even decades after their demolition.

Most cities have their ups and downs, and Marietta has been no exception. It has survived fire, war, depression, and in recent decades, the losses of many of its most notable buildings. Yet it continues to thrive, even in the midst of the worst economic downturn in seven decades as this book was written.

Marietta's downtown suffered three devastating fires in a single decade—the 1850s. It only got worse in the 1860s. As a result of the Civil War, many of the city's buildings were used as hospitals, nearby hillsides were scarred by two vast military cemeteries, and thanks to Gen. William Tecumseh Sherman's troops, most of downtown, including the courthouse, was left in smoldering ruins.

Marietta and Cobb County were so downtrodden following the war that it was not until seven years later that they could afford to build another courthouse. The city remained under such great economic duress that entire blocks facing the square sat covered with charred rubble into the 1890s, much like entire blocks of London, Berlin, and other European cities remained vacant for decades after the devastation of World War II.

Then, after eking through the Depression years, the arrival of the Bell Aircraft plant during World War II brought previously unimaginable opportunities and wealth to Marietta and seemingly solidified downtown's status as the commercial hub of the county. But it was not to be.

The advent of shopping malls and Interstate 75 siphoned shoppers and retailers away, and what followed was a three-decade descent for downtown. As shoppers headed elsewhere, Glover Park in Marietta Square became most notable, not for its fountain, but for the sizeable numbers of homeless and day laborers who congregated there each morning, courtesy of a nearby shelter and a day-labor pickup point. Few people traveled to downtown Marietta except those who needed to be there. With only a handful of restaurant and nightlife options near the square, at times downtown resembled a ghost town.

The election of lawyer Bob Flournoy Jr. as mayor in 1981 was the turning point for the square and downtown's fortunes. Flournoy, working closely with powerful state representative Joe Mack Wilson, launched a campaign to revitalize the square, exclaiming that he planned to "restore it to the grandeur that it never had!" He kept his word, spearheading an effort that generated $1 million in contributions and gave the redesigned and renovated Glover Park just what it needed to help regain its status as the focal point of the city. Among the donors to that campaign were Academy Award–winning actors Paul Newman and wife Joanne Woodward, a Marietta native.

With the advantage of hindsight, it can also be said that the opening of Theatre in the Square in 1982 was nearly as important as the renovation of Glover Park. The theater brought a steady stream of patrons to downtown, even in the theater's early years. The theatergoers did what theatergoers do around the world: go out to eat beforehand and perhaps have a drink afterward. Thus the theater provided a continual flow of customers for existing square eateries and fueled the development of additional ones.

Unfortunately, the square's downturn during the 1960s and 1970s went hand-in-hand with the gradual demolition of a 17-square-block area on the east and north sides of the downtown area. This change was a mixed blessing at best. The urban renewal of the early 1940s had been welcome and had erected the Clay Homes public housing project on the site of the city's previously biggest and most squalid slum, "Hollandtown," also known as "Green Street." Thousands of the city's poorest African American residents lived in shanties without indoor plumbing in conditions akin to something out of a Charles Dickens novel. But the renewals of the 1960s and 1970s robbed Marietta of some of its most notable historical and architectural treasures. Those losses included the old Marietta City Hall, the Waterman Street School, the Haynes Street School, the Lemon Street High School (for African Americans), the old freight depot, and the county administration building constructed of stone by Works Progress Administration workers during the Great Depression.

The razing of those buildings was eclipsed by the most striking act of civic vandalism of all—the late 1960s demolition of the Romanesque courthouse that had anchored Marietta Square for the previous century and, to paraphrase Churchill, had shaped the city. It was and is an irreplaceable loss.

If there was a silver lining to the city's defacement, it was the construction that ensued. A succession of county and city offices, court buildings, and banks were constructed, generating an ever-growing corps of workers to patronize downtown eateries and stores. The workers were a lifeline between the square's earlier days and its 1990s–2000s revival.

Unfortunately, most of the new buildings that replaced those that were previously demolished were less than notable from an architectural standpoint, tending to be designed in a modernistic, "fortress" style. Exceptions have included the handsome state court building on East Park Square and the old Cobb Federal Savings and Loan building with its unusual scalloped facade, which in recent years has been used as a county government office building but now is slated to be replaced with a parking deck.

Downtown Marietta has revived itself. In the early 1980s, few of even Marietta's most optimistic boosters would have believed that it would have transformed itself so dramatically. But it did, thanks to the political leadership of Mayors Flournoy and Joe Mack Wilson and to the dawning realization that though Marietta Square would never again be the county's retail hub, it could serve as a focal point for special events such as parades, political rallies, food festivals, art shows, and antique shows, which were capable of drawing tens of thousands of people. People who attend such events, explore the specialty and antique shops around the square, patronize the growing coterie of restaurants, or attend a show at Theatre in the Square or the reopened Strand Theatre quickly realize the uniqueness of downtown Marietta.

With the revitalization of the Strand, the square is looking better than ever as this book goes to press. The theater, a 1935-vintage art deco jewel, is the subject of a $4 million public/private renovation after a decades-long fallow period. Its offerings and bright lights bring new energy and excitement to downtown.

In another growing development, ground was broken as this book went to press for a new $63-million Cobb Superior Court Building featuring a design that consciously mimics that of the one demolished four decades ago. Unfortunately, it is not being erected on the site of the old courthouse but three blocks away at the foot of a hill where the grandeur of its soaring clock tower will be muted. The fact that it is a near–carbon copy of the older courthouse marks both a welcome departure from the uninspiring governmental architecture of so much of downtown and recognition that tearing down the old courthouse was one of the biggest mistakes in the county's history.

Indeed, two of the most notable events in Marietta's 175th year were the renovation and reopening of the Strand Theatre and the virtual recreation of the lamented old courthouse. These events bode well not just for the city's future but for the continued appreciation of its unique past—and for the possibility that like their forbearers, its buildings will continue to help shape our outlooks and attitudes.

CHAPTER 1

MARIETTA SQUARE AND NEARBY

Cotton was still king in rural Cobb in the 1940s, and it was not unusual for farmers to bring their bales to town via mule or their produce to sell at the farmer's market along Glover Park in the square. A young Bill Kinney of the *Marietta Journal* took this photograph on West Park Square. (Then image courtesy of Marietta Museum of History.)

The focal point of Glover Park in Marietta Square is now the fountain, as it was a century ago when this stereograph (at right) was taken. The present fountain dates to the square's $1-million face-lift in the 1980s under Mayor Bob Flournoy Jr. Actors Paul Newman and his wife, Joanne Woodward, a Marietta native, donated to the drive. (Then image courtesy of Marietta Museum of History.)

The Mannings were among Cobb's early settlers, and their descendants include the late Superior Court judge James Manning. The family owned a dry-goods store on the north side of the square on the present site of Efe's Turkish restaurant when the above photograph was taken in the early 1900s. From left to right in earlier photograph are Henry S. Manning, John Manning, two unidentified, Lawrence Manning, and Bob Manning. From left to right in the modern picture of Efe's Turkish restaurant are Mustafa Demirkok, Sami Ersenal, Jose Garcia, owner Hakan Senka, and Sera Johnson. (Then image courtesy of Aymar Manning.)

Mariettans turned out en masse for the 1912 dedication of the bronze statue of U.S. Senator Alexander Stephens Clay of Marietta, who died in office in November 1910. The statue originally stood on the east side of the square facing south but was moved to the west side and reoriented to face east during the 1980s renovation. Clay and Johnny Isakson remain the only two Cobb residents ever elected to the Senate. (Then image courtesy of Marietta Museum of History.)

The 1969 photograph (below) of the southeastern area of the square is most notable for what is missing: the Victorian-era Cobb Courthouse, newly demolished. The above photograph shows the office building that replaced it and the gazebo added to Glover Park during the mid-1980s renovations. Partly obscured by the tree at left in the earlier photograph is the statue of U.S. Senator A. S. Clay, which was moved to the west side of the square after the makeover. (Then image courtesy of Joe McTyre/Marietta Museum of History.)

Cosby's Drug Store, originally occupied by the city's first pharmacist, William Root, sat at the corner of Root Street and North Park Square. As the signs indicate, Cosby's also offered grass seed, garden seed, and school books. The smaller sign at left advertises cold soda. To the right is E. M. Northcutt's Dry Goods, Notions, and Shoes. (Then image courtesy of Marietta Museum of History.)

The Root Street–North Park Square corner has been the site of pharmacies since the city's earliest days, including Hodges Drug Company in the 1950s. Two of its deliverymen are pictured above. Hodges' location just down the block from the city's two theaters—the Cobb, at right, and the Strand, just out of picture to the right—made it a popular hangout during that era. The site today is Sugar Cakes patisserie. (Then image courtesy of Marietta Museum of History.)

This undated but probably early-20th-century shot (above) of the interior of the Hodges Drug store, on the north side of the square, gives an intimate view of a pharmacy in that era. The red, white, and blue bunting and numerous flags indicate the store was decorated for a patriotic occasion. Sugar Cakes, a French-style patisserie, now occupies the building. Sugar Cakes owner Ted Arpon is pictured below. (Then image courtesy of Marietta Museum of History.)

Below, the northeast side of Marietta Square looked like this following a fire on Halloween 1932 on the site of the future Strand Theatre. The three black lines above the burned-out buildings were part of the overhead electrical-wire system that powered the old Marietta-to-Atlanta trolley. Today these buildings are occupied by Three Bears Café and Efe's restaurant. (Then image courtesy of Marietta Museum of History.)

The 1903 photograph below shows farmers with their cotton bales on South Park Square looking east toward the old courthouse, the arched entryway of which is just visible through the trees at left rear. Piled in the street at right rear are items saved from the fire that destroyed the Elmwood Hotel. (Then image courtesy of Marietta Museum of History.)

This block on the southeast quadrant of the square stood vacant for more than 30 years after being burned by Sherman's troops. The three-story Elmwood Hotel was finally built on the quadrant just before 1900 and burned down just a few years later. Since then, the block has housed a variety of retailers. (Then image courtesy of Marietta Museum of History.)

This early-20th-century postcard (above) faces the southeast corner of the square toward Atlanta Street. A trolley car is just barely visible, as are a number of horses and carriages. At far left is the bell tower atop the city fire station on Atlanta Street, and just to its right is the much larger steeple of First Methodist Church of Marietta. Both are now gone. (Then image courtesy of Marietta Museum of History.)

Snow and ice storms are rare in Marietta, but this one in 1936 was notable. Below, a jalopy is ensnared in ice-laden power lines on Atlanta Street near the Gulf station (note "That Good GULF Gasoline" sign). Across the street is the former First Methodist Church building, which may date to the 1840s. It later was used as a Catholic church, an opera house, and then a car repair garage. More recently, it housed the Marietta Lighting Company. (Then image courtesy of Marietta Museum of History.)

The stretch of Atlanta Street between Waverly Way and Waterman Street has long been home to apartments and boardinghouses. This one on the west side of the street was heavily damaged by fire in the 1920s, and—minus its top floor, which was too heavily damaged to save—has served in recent decades as an office building. (Then image courtesy of Marietta Museum of History.)

The Atlanta Northern Railway line offered all-day trolley service from Marietta Square to Atlanta via Smyrna starting in 1905. Ridership fell sharply in the years after World War II, and with paved roads becoming more prevalent, the service was converted to buses. The trolley operation ended on January 31, 1947. In the photograph above, workers remove the trolley rails from Atlanta Street, with the old courthouse in the background at left. (Then image courtesy of Marietta Museum of History.)

Another view of Atlanta Street shows the trolley rails being removed. A comparison with the modern view (below) shows the streetscape has changed little during the ensuing six decades, aside from the signage and the kinds of businesses that line the road. In the distance across the square is the Strand Theatre, still the finest in Cobb County in the late 1940s. (Then image courtesy of Marietta Museum of History.)

It was shopping day in the early 1940s for these women crossing Powder Springs Street at Whitlock Avenue (below). At left on the corner is Crescent Furniture, and across Whitlock at right is the Brumby Press/*Cobb County Times* office, currently the Gone with the Wind Museum. Further down are Anderson Chevrolet at left and Guest Ford at right. The Crescent Furniture building is now the Marietta Pizza Company. (Then image courtesy of Marietta Museum of History.)

The First National Bank Building, at the corner of South Park Square and Powder Springs Street, was built in 1917 and was still new when the photograph below was taken in the 1920s. The building replaced the old Masonic lodge, one of the few buildings on the square to survive the fires set by Sherman's troops in November 1864. The bank expanded in 1957 and extended its marble facade. The building is currently used for offices. (Then image courtesy of Marietta Museum of History.)

Northcutt Automobiles, for years the city's premier car dealership, was headquartered on Powder Springs Street in the 1920s and eventually encompassed most of the block. Note the gas pump beneath the *O* in "Northcutt" on the sign. The tenants in the building, which has changed minimally from the outside, include Theatre in the Square's Alley Stage and the Marietta Wine Market. (Then image courtesy of Marietta Museum of History.)

Lindsey-Galt Furniture Company's showroom was on Whitlock Avenue, a half block off the square, for decades. In the photograph above, the building—a block away—on Powder Springs Street, next to the Southern Bell building, served as one of the company's annexes. Another was in the old Grapette warehouse, now the Krystal parking lot on Whitlock Avenue. After a period in the late 1990s as the Moonlight Spa massage parlor, the building seen below now houses the Natural Fitness store. (Then image courtesy of Jan Galt Russell.)

The economy of Marietta and Cobb County revolved around cotton for more than a century, as epitomized in the 1890s photograph below, taken facing north on West Park Square. Currently, the economy of downtown Marietta revolves around tourism, with a calendar that includes May-retta Daze, Art in the Park, and Taste of Marietta, during which the photograph above was taken in 2009. (Then image courtesy of Marietta Museum of History.)

On a sleepy-looking morning around 1928, an elderly man sits on a window ledge reading a newspaper on West Park Square facing Marietta Square. Note the traffic bucket in the middle of the intersection. Directional signs have progressed since then. Businesses on the west side of the square in that era included the Western Union telegraph office and Collins Brothers Druggists. (Then image courtesy of Marietta Museum of History.)

Marietta Square was still the epicenter of Cobb retailing in 1953, when the photograph above was taken. The stores on the west side of the square included Williams Drugs, Irving's Five and Dime, and Mother and Kiddie Shoes. The photograph below from the same location shows crowds at the 2009 Taste of Marietta. (Then image courtesy of Marietta Museum of History.)

Marietta Square was at low ebb in the late 1970s and early 1980s, when the photograph above was taken. The square's retailers and customers were leaving for nearby malls. Glover Park had not been restored yet, hence the lack of fencing and landscaping. Among the stores staying afloat were Vales Card and Gift Shop, the Jo-Ann shop, the Cozy Kitchen Ice Cream Parlor, and Leiter's clothing store. (Then image courtesy of Marietta Museum of History.)

Glover Park was another reminder of downtown's declining days in that era. The park was rundown and a hangout for the homeless thanks to a neighboring shelter and day-labor pickup point. At left in the photograph below are the remains of Friedman's Jewelers, the current site of Hemingway's eatery. On Depot Street is the Kennesaw House prior to its restoration. (Then image courtesy of Philip Goldstein.)

Watermelons were in season when this photograph was taken during the early 1940s outside of the Colonial Grocery. For years, the grocery faced Cherokee Street at Hansell Street, two blocks north of the square. The store was bulldozed in the late 1970s. Currently, the site is a parking lot for First Baptist Church of Marietta. (Then image courtesy of Marietta Museum of History.)

House of Lu restaurant is currently located a half-block off the square on Cherokee Street. The building housed the rhythm and blues club One Step Down in the mid-1980s, when this photograph was taken. Previously it was a rock venue, the Strand Cabaret, hosting acts like REM and Guadalcanal Diary. A century earlier, the building was a warehouse for guano, a vital ingredient in the process of tanning leather at nearby tanneries. (Then image courtesy of Dr. Tom Scott.)

By 1905, the House of Lu building was a cabinet shop and later—as the sign painted on the wall attests—Shorty's Shoe Shop. Also note the faded soft drink sign. The House of Lu building appears to have survived the 1930 fire that gutted Najjar's Department Store, which previously stood on the site of the present-day Strand Theatre at right. (Then image courtesy of Dr. Tom Scott.)

CHAPTER

2

ALONG THE TRACKS

Arguably the most historic structure in Marietta, the Kennesaw House dates to 1845 and was where Andrews' Raiders stayed the night before "the Great Locomotive Chase" in 1862. The house was visited by Sherman in 1864 and now houses the Marietta Museum of History. This photograph was taken in the 1940s. (Then image courtesy of Marietta Museum of History.)

The Kennesaw House served at various times as a hotel, tavern, post office, telegraph office, office building, and museum. The first floor housed several restaurants from the 1960s to 1980s, including one owned by former Atlanta Falcon Alex Hawkins. This photograph was taken from Depot Street in 1926, when the building was known as the Marietta Hotel. At left is the rear corner of the building that is now Hemingway's restaurant. (Then image courtesy of Marietta Museum of History.)

Originally the Fletcher Brothers' cotton warehouse, this building was erected in the early 1880s abutting the south wall of the Kennesaw House hotel, which can be seen on the left. After nearly a century as a warehouse, it was a restaurant for a couple of decades. The photograph above was taken in 1980, just prior to its renovation. The city's Gone with the Wind Museum opened in the building in 2002. (Then image courtesy of Marietta Museum of History.)

After Sherman's men burned Marietta's original train depot, a permanent replacement was not built until 1898 and featured stepped gables. The photograph above, from the 1940s, reiterates that Depot Street—between the train station and the Kennesaw House—was still an active street and railroad crossing. The crossing was later converted to pedestrian use and was the subject of a 1990s court battle after the railroad tried to close it. The city lost the fight. (Then image courtesy of Marietta Museum of History.)

Marietta's original train depot was torched by Sherman's men in 1864. A passenger depot was built in 1898 to replace it. Pictured below is the depot's interior around 1915. Seated at right is Albert Benson. The man on the left is unidentified. Note the spittoon on the floor. The depot is now the Marietta Welcome Center and is visited by thousands of people each year. Above, the Marietta Welcome Center staff is, from left to right, volunteers Carolyn Duncan and Beth Cooper and executive director Theresa Jenkins. (Then image courtesy of Marietta Museum of History.)

The Grapette Bottling Company once occupied this building along the railroad tracks. In the distance at right is the old city passenger depot—now the Marietta Welcome Center—with baggage carts lined up out front. Coincidentally, the Grapette operation was just a block from the site of the city's original Coca-Cola bottling operation on Husk Street. The Grapette building was demolished in the late 1970s for a Krystal fast food restaurant. (Then image courtesy of Marietta Museum of History.)

Dupre's is the oldest retail establishment in town, having occupied the corner of Whitlock Avenue by the railroad tracks since the Civil War era. Through the years, it has sold everything from dry goods to household appliances and even boats. It was converted to an antique emporium in 1995. The photograph above dates to the late 1940s and features what is probably an Army surplus jeep. (Then image courtesy of Marietta Museum of History.)

This bird's-eye view looks west on Whitlock Avenue. The Kennesaw House, the Marietta Paper Mill smokestack, and Kennesaw Mountain are the in the distance. The artist—who took obvious liberties with the size of the mountain—stood atop the old Masonic lodge building, a story higher than the structure there now. The drawing was on the cover of an 1887 booklet printed by the W&A Railroad to entice tourists. A surprising number of buildings in this view still stand. (Then image courtesy of Marietta Museum of History.)

CHAPTER

3

SCHOOLS AND CHURCHES

The 1924-vintage Marietta High School was already a couple of decades old when this shot was taken in the 1940s. In the foreground is the memorial to Alice McClellan Birney that was funded by donations from schoolchildren from around the country. Birney, a Marietta native, was founder in 1897 of the National Congress of Mothers, which later became the National Congress of Parents and Teachers, whose local units are known as PTAs. (Then image courtesy of Marietta Museum of History.)

The field of rolling oats is currently the Walker School, located along Cobb Parkway at Allgood Road. Fred Dunn owned the farm and also owned a grocery, feed, and seed store on Cherokee Street just off the square. He donated the acreage for the original Sprayberry High School, now the Walker School—one of the area's most highly regarded private schools. (Then image courtesy of Marietta Museum of History.)

The Waterman Street School for white students was the first school built after city voters approved free public schools in 1892. The city also spent $4,200 for a two-story wood building on Lemon Street for black students. The Waterman school was used through the 1960s and later burned. The Marietta Salvation Army barracks now occupy the site. In 1950, the city built a brick replacement for the Lemon Street School, by then a firetrap. (Then image courtesy of Marietta Museum of History.)

The old Marietta High School opened on Winn Street in 1924, a couple decades before the photograph above was taken. The cost of construction was $90,000. Among its graduates was future Academy Award–winner Joanne Woodward—best actress for *All About Eve*. The building is now Marietta Middle School. A new high school opened in 1998 on Whitlock Avenue. Its $57-million cost was a record at the time for Georgia high schools. (Then image courtesy of Marietta Museum of History.)

SCHOOLS AND CHURCHES

The Brumby Gym—home of the Marietta High School basketball Blue Devils—stood at the corner of Winn and Polk Streets. It had few peers in Georgia when it opened in 1940, but was outmoded by the 1980s and was replaced with this modern gym in 1992. This photograph below was taken just prior to its demolition. The school building is now home to Marietta Middle School. (Then image courtesy of Marietta Museum of History/Jan Galt Russell.)

The First United Methodist Church of Marietta stood at the corner of Atlanta and Anderson Streets from 1900 until 1966, when it moved to Whitlock Avenue. Pictured is the ground-breaking for its educational building in the 1950s. In the background is the steeple of the old courthouse a block away. Among those in attendance was *Marietta Journal* editor Bill Kinney, standing just to the right of the man in the dark suit holding a hat. (Then image courtesy of Marietta Museum of History.)

SCHOOLS AND CHURCHES

St. James Episcopal Church, pictured around 1900, was dedicated in 1843 and heavily vandalized by Yankee troops during the Civil War after its pastor refused to pray for the president of the United States. The body of Confederate general Leonidas Polk, prewar bishop of Louisiana, was brought to the church after he was killed at nearby Pine Mountain. The church was gutted by fire in 1964 but rebuilt based on the original plans. (Then image courtesy of Marietta Museum of History.)

In 1907, Crestview Baptist Church on Atlanta Street was founded as Second Baptist Church. The sanctuary was built in 1910, and funeral services were held in 1913 for murder victim Mary Phagan, whose family were members. She is buried just across the railroad tracks in the city cemetery. This sanctuary burned on Valentine's Day 1923. The present sanctuary was erected in 1992 and is now the sanctuary of Grace Pointe Church. (Then image courtesy of Crestview Baptist Church/ *Marietta Daily Journal*.)

CHAPTER 4

BUSINESS AND INDUSTRY

The Marietta Chair and Table Company on Church Street was founded by James Brumby, who had earlier founded Brumby Chair. The two buildings at left were originally connected by a catwalk. Marietta Chair went out of business just before World War I. Its buildings were renovated for office space in the early 1980s. (Then image courtesy of Marietta Museum of History.)

The ruins along Kennesaw Avenue were once part of the Wilder Tannery operation, opened in the 1800s by John Wilder and James Bolan Glover Sr. The Glover family also operated a large tannery about a mile south of town in the years before the Civil War. The tannery was near the Greek Revival plantation house built by the city's first mayor, John Heyward Glover. (Then image courtesy of Marietta Museum of History.)

In the 1890s, Robert Hull Northcutt founded the Marietta Knitting Company on Rose Lane, just north of downtown. The company employed 275 people and manufactured men's socks. It could produce 14,000 pairs of socks in a nine-hour workday, and during World War I, it received a contract from the U.S. Army to produce 436,000 pairs. The 75,000-square-foot plant, later known as Holeproof Hosiery, was converted to the McLaren Mill loft condominiums in the late 1990s. (Then image courtesy of Guy Northcutt Jr.)

The Glover Machine Works cranked out more than 200 steam locomotives during the early 1900s. After starting as a tool-and-die operation on Whitlock Avenue, the company moved to Butler Street in 1903. The Cobb Water Department has occupied the site since the demolition of the historic factory in the late 1990s. The factory's machinery and business records are now in the Southern Museum of Civil War and Locomotive History in Kennesaw. (Then image courtesy of Marietta Museum of History.)

BUSINESS AND INDUSTRY

This privately owned pedestrian bridge over the railroad tracks was built in 2009 by Marietta lawyer/developer Gary Eubanks as part of his Atlanta Northern Building project. On the other side of the tracks are the buildings of the former Marietta Chair Company, now Marietta Station.

The derelict building that once stood in the foreground below was part of the Marietta Ice Company, which formerly occupied the end of that block. (Then image courtesy of Marietta Museum of History.)

The steam-powered fire engine, the *Aurora*, was the pride of the Marietta Fire Department when it was purchased in 1879. The engine stayed in use until 1921. It is shown below in front of the Kennesaw Flour Mill/Marietta Paper Mill complex, which stood alongside the railroad tracks just north of Mill Street. The *Aurora* is now the centerpiece of the Marietta Fire Museum in the main city fire station on Haynes Street. (Then image courtesy of Marietta Museum of History.)

Until 1973, the *Marietta Journal* had its offices in the building at the corner of Anderson and Winters Streets, facing what was then the post office and is now the art museum. The photograph above was taken after the Brumby family, owners of the competing *Cobb County Times*, purchased the *Journal*. At right was "Hangman's Alley," the scene of a murder, a suicide, and a fatal fall. (Then image courtesy of Otis A. Brumby Jr.)

The Marietta Ice Company, later the Southland Ice Company, was built along the railroad tracks just south of Polk Street around 1900. Before electric refrigeration, the manufactured ice was sold to local customers and shipped to markets by rail. With the advent of home refrigeration, there was little need for the plant by the time the modern photograph was taken in the 1970s. (Then image courtesy of Marietta Museum of History.)

In 1949, Ken Stanton Music was founded, and in its early years, it was located in this antebellum warehouse along the tracks on Whitlock Avenue. The Darby and Maddox Printing Company was also located in the warehouse—previously the *Cobb County Times* building. Across the tracks is Lindsey Furniture (later Lindsey-Galt) in the old Grapette building. The renovated warehouse building now houses the Gone with the Wind Museum: Scarlett on the Square. (Then image courtesy of Marietta Museum of History.)

James Remley Brumby founded the Brumby Chair Company in 1875. By 1885, Brumby built a factory just north of Kennesaw Avenue along the railroad tracks, as seen in this old painting. The factory crafted large, sturdy Brumby rockers, which became an institution on Southern porches for more than a century. The company closed during World War II and was then resurrected in 1992 by newspaperman Otis A. Brumby Jr. (Then image courtesy of Otis A. Brumby Jr.)

The Brumby Chair Company was sold to former Marietta mayor L. M. "Rip" Blair in 1950, becoming the Blair Manufacturing Company. The expanded old factory was turned into the Brumby Loft apartments in the late 1990s. The footbridge at left over North Marietta Parkway dates to the early 2000s. (Then image courtesy of Marietta Museum of History.)

By the late 1950s and early 1960s, businesses were beginning to move to Marietta's suburbs. Among them was Marietta Federal Savings and Loan Association, which opened this branch on Roswell Street just east of Fairground Street. Across the street were the offices of the Cobb Chamber of Commerce, which has been in the Platinum Triangle area since the 1980s. (Then image courtesy of Marietta Museum of History.)

CHAPTER

5

HOMES

This 1850s house at the Butler Street crossing of the railroad tracks was home to 13-year-old Mary Phagan's grandfather. Her 1913 murder, and the ensuing 1915 lynching of her accused murderer Leo Frank, set off a chain of events that still haunts Marietta. The house stood empty in the early 2000s, and then became victim of arson as it was being restored. (Then image courtesy of Georgia Room/Cobb Library.)

The Gignilliat-Hutcheson House was located from the mid-1840s until the mid-1940s on Polk Street across the railroad tracks from St. James Episcopal Church. The body of Confederate general Leonidas Polk was brought here on its way to St. James after a shell at Pine Mountain killed him in 1864. His service was reportedly held on the grounds of the house. The house was demolished to make room for a lumberyard. (Then image courtesy of Marietta Museum of History.)

Marietta's first mayor, John Heyward Glover, built this cottage on Wright Street in 1848. Also in 1848, he built the Greek Revival–style Brushy Park plantation house—known to modern Mariettans as the old 1848 House Restaurant—3 miles south of town. His wife, Jane, complained it was too far from town, so he built another large house on Whitlock Avenue in front of this house, which was used as slave quarters. (Then image courtesy of Marietta Museum of History.)

This Church Street home was built in 1895 on the site of a former tanyard by Mills McNeel of the McNeel Marble Company—one of the county's largest employers at the time. Future inhabitants included State Supreme Court justice J. Harold Hawkins and the Claude Hamrick family, who named it Hamrick Hall. (Then image courtesy of Marietta Museum of History.)

The Galley House was formerly located just north of First Presbyterian Church of Marietta on Church Street and was erected in 1898 by Sam K. Dick. The home later served as a boardinghouse, and in 1963, it was purchased by the expanding church. Along with the other houses on the east side of Church Street between the church and Kennesaw Avenue, the Galley House was demolished and replaced with church parking. (Then image courtesy of Marietta Museum of History.)

In 1930, James Bolan Glover III built this brick home. The house was located on Whitlock Avenue a few doors west of the house built by his grandfather John Heyward Glover, Marietta's first mayor. It later was deeded to Aimee Dunwoody Glover Little, a descendant of several prominent Marietta families. Today it is the home of attorney Eric Welch. (Then image courtesy of Marietta Museum of History.)

The Northcutts and Winterses were two of Marietta's most prosperous early families. Two brothers of one of the families married two sisters of the other and built adjacent houses at the foot of Winters Street south of the square. In the foreground is the Northcutt House in late 1890s with the Winters House in the background. The Northcutt House burned in 1912 and was never rebuilt. Gibbs Auto, with co-owner Marc Gibbs in the foreground, now stands on its approximate site. (Then image courtesy of Guy Northcutt Jr.)

The Chamberlain House was built in 1888 atop a hill on Washington Avenue across the street from the Marietta National Cemetery. The cemetery is the final resting place for thousands of Union Civil War soldiers. The old house was torn down in the mid-2000s to accommodate the Washington Avenue Commons condominium project. (Then image courtesy of Marietta Museum of History.)

This late-1800s photograph depicts the home built by R. B. Bostwick in the 1840s. After the Battle of Kennesaw Mountain, the home served as a hospital and eventually was the county Department of Family and Children Services office. It was located just south of the Waterman Street School and was demolished in the 1970s for South Marietta Parkway (the Loop). An identical house built by Bostwick's brother, C. C. Bostwick, is on nearby Frasier Street. (Then image courtesy of Marietta Museum of History.)

The original Marietta Country Club site on Powder Springs Street was the location of the Georgia Military Institute before the Civil War. After the Battle of Kennesaw Mountain, it was a hospital and Union cavalry staging area before being burned by Sherman. It was the town ball field in late 1800s. Among those who played there was pioneering knuckleballer Nap Rucker of neighboring Crabapple. The club relocated to west Cobb in 1990. (Then image courtesy of Marietta Museum of History.)

CHAPTER 6

HERE AND THERE

The Atlanta Northern Railway started running in 1905, making it feasible for the first time for city residents to commute to Atlanta for work. In 1913, a trolley is pictured stopped in front of the old courthouse disgorging passengers. Five surreys with fringe on the top are parked alongside the trolley. (Then image courtesy of Marietta Museum of History.)

ERVIN PYLANT   R. FRED PYLANT

The Pylant Garage on Church Street north of the square was built to take advantage of the traffic on Church. In the pre-interstate 1930s, Church Street doubled as U.S. 41, the main traffic artery between Chicago and Florida. Today it is the headquarters of the Marietta Trolley Company.

From left to right in the photograph below are Melanie Richardson, Brad Quinlin, owners Brian and Cassandra Buckalew, Charlie Webb, and Kathleen Jones. (Then image courtesy of Marietta Museum of History.)

The Atlanta Northern Railway Company ran electric trolley cars from Atlanta to Marietta and back from 1905 to 1947. In this photograph, one of the trolley cars approaches the South Cobb Drive underpass just west of the Lockheed Martin plant. The overpass was built in 1942 at the same time the plant was constructed for Bell Aircraft during World War II. Today CSX Railroad trains run along nearly the same path. (Then image courtesy of Marietta Museum of History.)

The Western and Atlantic Railroad was crucial to Marietta's development. In this early-1940s photograph by newspaperman Bill Kinney, a steam locomotive heads south. The buildings on the right along Atlanta Street are long gone, as is the water tank and the high embankment next to the tracks. (Then image courtesy of Bill Kinney/Marietta Museum of History.)

The Marietta Fruit Stand began as just that—a fruit stand in the Elizabeth community—before morphing into a meat-and-three restaurant that was popular with workers from nearby Kennestone Hospital in the 1970s and 1980s. Jokingly known as "The Elizabeth Country Club," the unpretentious eatery was bulldozed in the 1990s for a road widening. The restaurant reopened in a storefront on Whitlock Avenue. The First Cherokee Bank now occupies the old fruit stand location. (Then image courtesy of Marietta Museum of History.)

HERE AND THERE

Not a scene likely to be repeated, local Tom Hodge was photographed in the early 1900s outside of W. T. Moscher's Candy Kitchen and ice cream emporium on the south side of the square, which probably explains the crowd of kids. Moscher's also held the distinction of being the first soda fountain in Cobb to serve Coca-Cola. The Australian Bakery currently occupies the old candy store. (Then image courtesy of Marietta Museum of History.)

The Roswell Street–Cobb Parkway intersection bore little resemblance in this early 1940s aerial view to the congested place it is today. The older photograph shows Roswell Street running top to bottom, toward Marietta, at the bottom of the page. The modern photograph includes local landmark The Big Chicken and depicts Roswell Street running right to left toward Marietta. The 1915 lynching of Leo Frank took place in a grove of trees near the upper right side of the older photograph. (Then image courtesy of Bill Kinney; now image courtesy of *Marietta Daily Journal*/Bret Gerbe.)

Leo Frank was convicted of murdering 13-year-old Mary Phagan of Marietta in his Atlanta factory, where she worked. In 1915, when the governor commuted his death sentence to life in prison, Mariettans kidnapped him from prison and hung him from this tree off Roswell Street. The tree, pictured at right with its trunk wrapped—most likely to protect it from souvenir-hunters—was felled in the 1970s for the I-75 underpass. (Then image courtesy of Marietta Museum of History.)

84

GOVERNMENT
BUILDINGS

The old courthouse loomed over Marietta Square for a century. The Stonewall Hotel, two doors away, was one of three downtown hotels in the 1940s. The steeple in the distance is from First Methodist Church. The courthouse and the other buildings on that side of the square were demolished in the late 1960s. (Then image courtesy of Marietta Museum of History.)

Marietta's police headquarters in the 1940s and 1950s was located on Powder Springs Street by the Southern Bell Building (above, at left), just a few steps from the previous city hall on Atlanta Street. The department moved to Lawrence Street in 1960. The current police headquarters houses 137 officers and 32 civilians, far more than would have fit into this building. That site is now a parking lot. (Then image courtesy of Marietta Museum of History.)

In this 1908 photograph is a ladder wagon from the Marietta Fire Department when it was housed on Atlanta Street a half-block off the square in a building topped with a 30-foot bell tower. One of the two fire horses was named Herbert after county solicitor general Herbert Clay. Clay was the son of Sen. A. S. Clay of Marietta. The heavily remodeled building currently houses Johnny McCracken's Irish Pub. (Then image courtesy of Marietta Museum of History.)

In 1909, the old Marietta post office building on Atlanta Street opened. According to old fire insurance maps, it was previously the site of "Negro Tenements." The post office served the city until a new office was built on Lawrence Street in 1963. After that it was the main Cobb Library until the late 1980s. In 2009, the newly restored building marked its 20th year as the Marietta/Cobb Museum of Art. (Then image courtesy of Marietta Museum of History.)

The current Cobb Civic Center/Anderson Theatre/Larry Bell Park complex on Fairground Street served as the county work farm (prison) during the early 20th century. Inmates tilled the farm's fields and, wearing balls and chains, worked on local roads. Pictured is the warden's house near the Fairground Street–Clay Street intersection. The old Dunaway Drugs/Kroger building can be seen through the fence in the distance. (Then image courtesy of Marietta Museum of History.)

Turner Chapel's vintage 1891 sanctuary building was in the midst of demolition when this photograph was taken in the early 1970s. A close look shows that its windows have been removed. The congregation met on Lawrence Street near Fairground Street from 1974 until 2005, when it built a church on North Marietta Parkway. The old church site was replaced by a bank that now houses the main county government offices. (Then image courtesy of *Marietta Daily Journal*.)

GOVERNMENT BUILDINGS

A knot of officials gathers at left for the ground-breaking of the county's public safety building, which soon replaced the two-story structure at right—the old Cobb jail. The jail was demolished in the late 1960s along with the courthouse. In the background is the steeple of the old First United Methodist Church, which was also demolished in the late 1960s. (Then image courtesy of Ernest Wester Collection, KSU Archives.)

GOVERNMENT BUILDINGS

Behind the old Fulton Federal bank building (at far left), there is currently a parking lot, which until the late 1960s was filled with houses and shade trees. Some of their remains are piled in the foreground of the then photograph. At far right is Turner Chapel A.M.E. Church (facing Lawrence Street), which was demolished shortly after this photograph was taken. (Then image courtesy of Ernest Wester Collection/KSU Archives.)

GOVERNMENT BUILDINGS

Cobb's first courthouse was a log cabin on the square. This building took its place. When a new Greek Revival courthouse was built in 1853, this courthouse was rolled down Washington Avenue on logs, and it is now the law offices of Bentley, Bentley, and Bentley. No photograph survives of the 1853 courthouse, which was burned by Sherman, but its columned ruins can be glimpsed in this 1867 photograph from the National Cemetery. (Both images courtesy of Marietta Museum of History.)

Cobb's fourth courthouse was built in 1872. Its original Greek Revival facade (at right) was given a more stylish Romanesque update in 1899. Its central tower was replaced with a more dominant steeple, as seen in this 1920s shot (below) as a city fire engine displays its water pump. The county demolished the courthouse in the late 1960s, claiming it was too small, and replaced it with a nondescript office building. (Both images courtesy of Marietta Museum of History.)

Destruction of the historic courthouse on the square is considered one of the gravest mistakes in the county's history. When the need arose for a new Superior Court Building in 2009, leaders made a conscious decision to let its design echo that of the departed one. In May 2009, ground was broken at the corner of Lawrence and Haynes Streets off the square for the $63-million courthouse, pictured in an artist's rendering (below). (Then image courtesy of Cobb County Government.)

www.arcadiapublishing.com

Discover books about the town where you grew up, the cities where your friends and families live, the town where your parents met, or even that retirement spot you've been dreaming about. Our Web site provides history lovers with exclusive deals, advanced notification about new titles, e-mail alerts of author events, and much more.

MADE IN THE USA

Arcadia Publishing, the leading local history publisher in the United States, is committed to making history accessible and meaningful through publishing books that celebrate and preserve the heritage of America's people and places. Consistent with our mission to preserve history on a local level, this book was printed in South Carolina on American-made paper and manufactured entirely in the United States.

This book carries the accredited Forest Stewardship Council (FSC) label and is printed on 100 percent FSC-certified paper. Products carrying the FSC label are independently certified to assure consumers that they come from forests that are managed to meet the social, economic, and ecological needs of present and future generations.

FSC
Mixed Sources
Product group from well-managed
forests and other controlled sources

Cert no. SW-COC-001530
www.fsc.org
© 1996 Forest Stewardship Council

Find Your Place in History.